Traditional
FLOWER REMEDIES

Traditional FLOWER REMEDIES

MARGARET CROWTHER

SIENA

WARNING

If you have a medical condition, or are pregnant, the information in this book should not be followed without consulting your doctor first. All guidelines, warnings and instructions should be read carefully *before* embarking on any of the treatments. Although the treatments suggested in this book are unlikely to produce adverse side effects, there are always exceptions to the rule. The treatments are taken at the reader's sole discretion.

The publisher cannot accept responsibility for injuries or damage arising out of a failure to comply with the above.

A Siena book
Siena is an imprint of Parragon Books

First published in Great Britain in 1996 by
Parragon Book Service Ltd
Units 13-17, Avonbridge Industrial Estate
Atlantic Road, Avonmouth
Bristol BS11 9QD

ISBN 0-75251-727-9

Printed in Great Britain
Produced by Kingfisher Design Services, London

Series Editor Jenny Plucknett
Series Design Pedro Prá-Lopez, Kingfisher Design Services

Medical Herbalist consultant Zoe Capernaros MA MNIMH
Illustrations Jill Moore
Plant illustrations pages 11, 13, 15, 17, 19 Wayne Ford
Typesetting/DTP Frances Prá-Lopez, Kingfisher Design Services

Contents

The Appeal of Flowers

F lowers have always had a special appeal for human beings and from the earliest days of civilization people have cultivated gardens and grown flowers. Many flowers have the power to heal and cure, but the pleasure they can give is also a tonic in itself, refreshing and revitalizing the spirits or soothing the mind after a busy day.

FLOWERS IN COUNTRY LORE

Well into the twentieth century, country wives traditionally grew their own favourite plants and gathered wild flowers from the fields and hedgerows to prepare them as remedies for every-day complaints and for other household uses. With the growth of modern science and changing ways of living these traditions have almost slipped into the past, but the more science investigates, the more it is found that there is often a good scientific reason for the effectiveness of the old traditional remedies.

FINDING THE INGREDIENTS

Everyone can enjoy the pleasure of experimenting with flower remedies. The simplest remedies require nothing more than the flowers themselves, fresh or dried, and many common flowering plants can be grown quite easily in gardens, or even window boxes, while dried flowers, both common and rare, are available from many health and drug stores as well as herbalists and other more specialist suppliers.

For some remedies, essential oils are needed. These cannot be prepared at home, but are widely available and wonderfully aromatic, as they are extracted in minute quantities from hand-picked flowers. But they are wonderfully potent and are used by the drop, so that a little goes a long way. Other simple ingredients, such as cocoa-butter, vinegar and honey, are cheap and readily obtainable, and for an introduction to the power of flowers, some useful flower preparations can even be bought ready-made.

Using Flowers Today

With home-grown flowers or bought dried ingredients, we can still use flowers today to maintain our health, freshen our homes and soothe our senses in the traditional way.

Do not expect miraculous results from flowers. They are gentle on the body and their effect may be a little slower than that of modern medicine. The bonus is that they they are pleasant to use, have no damaging side effects and are not habit forming.

PROTECTING THE COUNTRYSIDE

Many wild flowers are now protected by law, and many more once common plants have become rare, thanks to the spread of towns and suburbs, the use of herbicides, the building of roads and the increase in road traffic. Growing your own flowers for use in remedies is much more satisfying than depleting the countryside of its remaining flowers. Seeds of many wild flowers can be bought and the plants can be found on sale in garden centres or hunted out from specialist suppliers.

WARNING

Do not use flowers which have been treated with insecticides or herbicides or those growing near to roads with more than very light traffic.

Using Flowers Safely

Flower remedies are basically safe and harmless. However, some individuals can prove sensitive to some flower ingredients, and if any adverse reaction occurs you should discontinue use immediately. It goes without saying that you should first be absolutely sure that you have correctly identified the plant when picking your own flowers, or that when buying you obtain your materials from a reputable source.

* Observe scrupulous hygiene when preparing your remedies.

* If your symptoms continue, always seek professional medical advice. Do not take a remedy for more than 2-3 weeks unless advised to do so by a medical herbalist or other qualified professional.

* For children under 6, give one third of the adult dose. For children aged 6-15, give half the adult dose. Do not treat children under the age of 6 with essential oils.

Where mentioned in this book 1 tsp = 1 x 5ml spoon and 1 tbsp = 1 x 15ml spoon

---

WARNING

If you are pregnant, seek medical advice before using flower remedies.

— 1 —
Rose

ROSA SPECIES

The rose has always been loved for its perfume, but it is also useful medicinally. The essential oil is used by aromatherapists to treat anxiety and depression, and has also been successful in the treatment of premenstrual tension and irregular periods, headaches and insomnia. In beauty therapy it is particularly good for aging and sensitive skins.

Rose hips, which are astringent and rich in vitamin C, are used in preparations for colds, dysentery and diarrhoea, and were formerly used to treat and prevent scurvy. Medical herbalists consider the Rose to be a general tonic that is uplifting and good for the heart, as well as for depression.

WARNING

Despite its mildness and calming effect, some aromatherapists advise that it is best not to use Rose oil during the first three months of pregnancy.

PREPARING AND USING ROSES

Distilled Rose water can be purchased from pharmacists and drug stores, Rose essential oil can be found among aromatherapy oils, and dried Rose petals are available from herbalists and other suppliers. You can also make preparations using your own scented Roses – red Roses are said to be the best, see page 25. Gather the flowers for use on a dry day, after the dew has dried and when the buds are just opening.

Rose Remedy

Rose honey is a traditional remedy for a sore throat.
Make a strong infusion, see pages 31-32, of 2 tbsp of fresh Rose petals to a cup of boiling water. Cover and allow to cool. Strain the liquid, pressing the petals well. Heat with honey in an enamelled pan and allow to boil. Pot in a clean glass jar (allow to cool before putting on the lid). Take a teaspoonful as required, either neat or mixed with a little hot water in a glass.

Chamomile

·

Roman Chamomile CHAMAEMELUM NOBILE
German Chamomile MATRICARIA RECUTITA/
CHAMOMILLA RECUTITA

Chamomile is a daisy-like plant with feathery leaves and is a traditional folk remedy for many day-to-day complaints. The flowers are used fresh or dried and until not long ago were grown or gathered wild by country housewives. The plant is also said to be a favourite of the gypsies, who believe that it can prevent nightmares. Either German or Roman Chamomile can be used in simple remedies. Wild chamomile is now becoming increasingly rare and should not be picked.

PREPARING AND USING CHAMOMILE

This gentle, versatile herb is cleansing and healing, sedative and tonic.
It is used as a safe, mild painkiller for headaches, fever and 'flu, and in the treatment of period problems, nausea, indigestion and insomnia.
It also makes a good general tonic and will calm inflammation and swelling. Chamomile is so gentle that it is good for soothing numerous children's complaints, from feverishness to tummy upsets, and is equally suitable for treating the elderly.

Aromatherapists use the essential oil for skin ailments such as acne, boils, and dry skin (it is especially good for sensitive skins), to calm the mind and to treat headaches, migraine and insomnia. Chamomile lotion is a beauty treatment for fair hair and can also be used as a skin tonic.

The dried flowers are sold by herbalists and in health and drug stores, and sachets for tea are widely available. Chamomile preparations such as herbal ointments and hair treatments can also be bought. If you grow your own Chamomile you can use the fresh flowers and leaves and keep a jar of dried flowers ready for winter use.

Chamomile remedy

To soothe sensitive skin and aid relaxation add two Chamomile tea bags to the bath water.

Marigold

CALENDULA OFFICINALIS

Marigold or Calendula is often known as Pot Marigold, and at one time its petals were a standard addition to any cooking pot. The best Marigold for use in remedies is the single, bright gold type, rather than double and 'art shade' varieties. In early days the flower was known as Goldes but in medieval times it was associated with the Virgin Mary and began to be called Mary's Gold or Marigold.

PREPARING AND USING MARIGOLDS

Marigolds had many uses in folk medicine and are still widely used today. Marigold infusion soothes and heals the skin and is used externally for chapped hands, scars, eczema and other skin troubles. As a cold compress it can reduce the inflammation of sprains and pulled muscles (it absorbs heat from the body and should be renewed when it becomes hot). Medical herbalists use Marigold to treat liver, arteries and veins, including varicose veins, for fever, and as a digestive tonic. It also has anti-fungal properties. Diluted tincture of Marigold promotes the healing of wounds, including festering wounds. A Marigold flower infusion, see page 31, helps to control thread (broken) veins, and Marigold is a traditional ingredient of complexion creams and lotions.

Preparations containing Marigold extract can be bought from pharmacists and drug stores, herbalists and health stores, and herbalists sell dried petals and Calendula tincture. This is a very easy plant to grow and the flowers can be used fresh, by squeezing the juice directly onto the skin, or made into a lotion, tincture or salve. Fresh or dried petals can be made into an infusion or added to other herbal teas.

Marigold remedy

The pain and swelling of wasp and bee stings is said to be relieved by squeezing the juice from a Marigold flower over the affected area. It s also said that Marigold juice can be used to remove warts.

Sweet Violet

VIOLA ODORATA

The pretty wild Violet is one of the earliest flowers of spring. Violets were once used to make edible delicacies and sweetmeats, and have long been associated with beauty and used in perfumery. In earlier times the flowers were used to impart their fragrant oils to the water used for washing and bathing and their gentle scent is calming and soothing.

PREPARING AND USING VIOLETS

An infusion of Violet flowers can be drunk as a tea or applied as a compress to soothe headaches. It was also said to calm the nerves, soothe restlessness and even improve the memory. The flowers are both expectorant and laxative, and crystallized violets were once used for consumption, while syrup of violets was used to treat constipation in children. An infusion of the flowers can make a cooling eye wash for inflamed eyes, and a poultice of the fresh leaves can be very soothing to bruises. In some countries, medical herbalists prescribe the plant for skin problems such as boils, abscesses and pimples, and for respiratory complaints.

Violets are increasingly rare, so do not pick wild Violets. Seeds can be bought for growing the plant at home.

Violet remedy

For headaches, steep 3 tsp of fresh flowers and leaves or 1 tsp of dried flowers in a cup of boiling water. Cover and allow to infuse for 15 minutes. Strain. Drink cool, one cup daily, a mouthful at a time, or make in the same proportions and apply to the temples as a cold compress.

WARNING

Do not store Violet infusions for more than 24 hours.
Prolonged continuous internal use of large doses can cause nausea and vomiting.

Lavender

· ·

LAVANDULA ANGUSTIFOLIA, L. OFFICINALIS, L. SPICA

Lavender has been used since the time of the Ancient Romans, and apart from its aromatic fragrance it has strong antiseptic and therapeutic properties. Originally a plant from the mountainous areas of the Mediterranean coast, it is now grown all over the world. Lavender has always been of great importance in perfumes and toiletries and in earlier times it was used as a condiment to flavour food, with its medicinal properties as a bonus.

PREPARING AND USING LAVENDER

This is one of the pleasantest and safest flower remedies for external use and is used by herbalists and aromatherapists alike. Herbalists mainly use Lavender dried and as a tincture, and aromatherapists use the essential oil from the flowers. This blends well with many other oils, and is an important element in any First Aid box. It soothes minor cuts and burns, sprains and sunburn.

Lavender can ease physical or mental tiredness and relieve insomnia. It is used externally to treat fainting, headaches and nervous complaints, sunstroke and all manner of skin troubles. It may also be medically prescribed for respiratory problems, poor circulation, nausea and vomiting. Taken internally, diluted tincture of Lavender aids the digestion.

Up to 5 drops of Lavender oil can be dropped onto a sugar cube as an internal remedy, or a few flower spikes can be eaten raw in salad. For external use, the oil can be used on its own or mixed with a carrier oil or water.

Lavender remedies

To help to heal skin rashes or minor burns and wounds add 6 drops of essential oil of Lavender to a bath.

As a mouth wash for bad breath use Lavender water. Swill the water around the mouth, then spit out.

Geranium

PELARGONIUM ODORANTISSIMUM

The scented garden Geranium, properly called Pelargonium, is the source of the Geranium oil generally used by aromatherapists. Medical herbalists more frequently use species of the wild Geranium, American Cranesbill, *Geranium maculatum*.

USING GERANIUM

Geranium (Pelargonium) oil is extracted from the leaves, rather than the flowers, and is used by aromatherapists to treat a range of problems. Both relaxing and stimulating, it can be tried for depression and nervous tension. The best oil comes from Rose Geranium and is similar to oil of Roses, with which it can be mixed. It is very beneficial to the skin and can be used for skin problems such as dry eczema, shingles and ringworm and to treat minor burns. Wild Geranium is astringent and extracts from the plant can be used internally to treat diarrhoea, gastric disorders and colic, but only on the advice of a medical herbalist.

Geranium remedy

To cleanse, refresh and tone the skin mix 2 drops of essential oil of Geranium with 1 tsp of Sweet Almond carrier oil and apply on cotton wool.

Clary Sage

SALVIA SCLAREA

This member of the sage family is grown in gardens for its pretty pale blue, purple and white flower heads and is sometimes known just as Clary.

USING CLARY SAGE

Clary Sage was used as a herbal remedy in the middle ages for its general curative properties. It is still sometimes prescribed by medical herbalists for throat and respiratory infections, but it is the highly aromatic oil from the flowers and leaves that is now commonly used. This is an important ingredient in perfumery, and is increasingly valued by aromatherapists, who find that it is calming and euphoric, so that it can ease depression and treat panic states. Clary Sage is tonic and antiseptic and a massage with 3-5 drops of Clary Sage essential oil per 1 tbsp of Sweet Almond oil produces a feeling of well-being. The same mix can be used locally to treat inflamed or oily skin, boils, acne and dandruff.

Clary Sage remedy

As a soothing and stimulating pick-me-up add 6 drops of the essential oil to a warm bath.

Jasmine

Common White Jasmine JASMINUM OFFICINALE
Spanish Jasmine JASMINUM GRANDIFLORUM

Throughout the summer Jasmine produces headily scented starry white flowers which are the source of Jasmine oil. The oil used today is generally extracted from commercially grown Spanish Jasmine, which is similar but more bushy and with larger flowers than Common Jasmine.

USING JASMINE

Today it is the essential oil that is mainly used. Known for its exotic and uplifting perfume, it is used in massage, as a general tonic and calmative. Aromatherapists may use Jasmine oil to treat anxiety, postnatal depression, painful periods, dry and inflamed skin, coughs and hoarseness. It is also said to be an aphrodisiac, no doubt because of its calming effect, which helps overcome tension, anxiety and stress.

Jasmine essential oil helps to balance the production of sebum, which keeps the skin supple, and is beneficial to both dry and oily skins. It is costly to buy, but a little goes a long way.

Jasmine remedy

To help cure muscular spasm and sprains massage the affected area with 2 drops of Jasmine essential oil mixed with 1 tbsp of Sweet Almond oil.

Ylang-ylang

CANANGA ODORATA

Ylang-ylang flowers grow on a tropical tree, originating from parts of Asia but now grown commercially in other tropical areas. The flowers produce an exotically scented oil that has long been known in the East but has only recently come into use in the West. It has an unmistakable, sweet and strongly floral scent, which is calming and relaxing and which can produce a feeling of euphoria.

USING YLANG-YLANG

The oil is traditionally used in perfumery and cosmetics and it is now also used by aromatherapists to treat depression, nervous and mental tension and insomnia. It is said to be stimulating for poor circulation and good for the skin. It helps to regulate the production of sebum and so is beneficial in the treatment of both very dry and very oily skins and can be very helpful in cases of acne. The sensuous and uplifting scent is said to be aphrodisiac and certainly produces a feeling of well-being. Like Jasmine, Ylang-ylang essential oil is an expensive but luxurious treat.

Ylang-ylang remedy

To make a nourishing face oil for normal to oily skin mix 2 drops of Ylang-ylang with 1 tsp of Sweet Almond or Apricot kernel oil .

— 2 —

Growing Flowers

Many beneficial and beautiful flowers can easily be grown
for use at home, in a garden, in tubs and containers on a patio
or balcony, and even in a small window box. Among the
plants mentioned on pages 10-23, the following are
easy to grow for use in flower remedies:
ROSES • MARIGOLDS • VIOLETS,
CLARY SAGE • LAVENDER • CHAMOMILE • GERANIUMS.

WILD FLOWERS

Unless you have a good knowledge of wild flower species it is better not to
pick them, as many are now rare and protected by law. However, if you are
sure that you have correctly identified a plant that can legally be picked, and
you find it growing in profusion, follow the guidelines below when collecting:

- Pick the stems or flower heads without damaging the rest of the plant.

- Never pick more than you really need, and do not pick flowers unless
  you know that you can deal with them as soon as you get home.

- For your own safety, do not pick flowers where insecticides or herbicides
  may have been used or those growing near to roads with more than very
  light traffic.

ROSES

Strongly scented Roses are the best to choose, see below.
Roses bought in containers may be planted at any time of year,
although late autumn or early spring are best.

Planting Roses

❋ Plant Roses in well-prepared soil that is not too poor or sandy.

❋ Dig a hole a little wider and deeper than the pot. Stand the pot
in the hole to check the size. After planting, the earth should
come a little higher up the stem than the compost in the pot.

❋ Fork the earth in the bottom of the hole and mix in a handful of
general fertilizer.

❋ Remove the rose from its pot and loosen the roots a little around
the edges with a small fork. Place in the planting hole.

❋ Replace the soil, firming it gently between the roots as you go.
Firm around the plant and water well.

SOME ROSES TO CHOOSE FROM

CENTIFOLIA, PROVENCE or CABBAGE ROSES (*Rosa x centifolia*)
DAMASK ROSES (*Rosa damascena*) • DOG ROSE (*Rosa canina*)
GALLICA ROSES (*Rosa gallica*) • RUGOSA ROSES (*Rosa rugosa*).
Do not use garden hybrids in flower remedies.

MARIGOLDS

Marigolds can be grown easily from seed and will seed themselves after
the first year. Sow the seeds in spring in trays of seed compost.
Keep moist but do not over-water.

Growing from seed

❋ When the seedlings are large enough to handle, transfer them to a tray of
potting compost, setting them 5cm (2in) apart so that they can spread.

❋ When the young plants are bushy, transfer them to pots, window boxes or
garden beds.

❋ The seeds may also be sown outside, directly where they are to flower.

VIOLETS

Wild Violet seeds are available from some seed companies.
They germinate best when covered with just a dusting of compost and
kept out of the light. The plants will flourish in soil that has been
well dug and manured the previous autumn.

Increasing plant numbers

❋ Sow the Violet seeds in trays of seed compost in spring or late summer.

❋ Put the young plants into a well-manured bed the following year.

❋ Lift and divide established plants in autumn when they become too
spreading. This will give you more plants and increase flower production.

CLARY SAGE

Clary Sage is grown from seeds sown directly into a sunny border.
Sow the seeds in spring when the earth has warmed up.
Thin out the young plants and space them 30cm (12in) apart.

LAVENDER

Lavender is best grown from cuttings and needs light, well-drained soil.
It is equally at home in a garden bed, or in pots on the patio. Start with
a container-grown plant, then take cuttings from the woodier young
shoots to replace it when it becomes too leggy. Grow Lavender
in a sunny part of the garden or patio.

CHAMOMILE

Chamomile is also best grown from cuttings taken in late spring.
Alternatively, divide plants in autumn. Start with young plants obtained
from herb suppliers. Grow Chamomile in a sunny part
of the garden or patio.

GERANIUMS

Geraniums (Pelargoniums) can be grown from seed in a greenhouse,
but it is easier to buy young plants. Cuttings taken from these in late
summer will sometimes root readily in water to provide
new plants for the following season.

Gathering, Drying & Storing Flowers

Normally flowers should be gathered just as they become fully open, and they should always be picked if possible in a period of dry, sunny weather. Allow the morning dew to dry off the flowers first, but pick them in the morning before the sun reaches its highest point. Choose flowers in perfect condition, and cut the flower stalks low down, to leave the plant unspoilt and to prevent the flowers from drying out as you pick them.

Dry the flowers as soon as possible after they have been gathered to get the full benefits of the oils they contain. Tempting though it may be to dry flowers outside in the sun in summery weather it is much better to dry them indoors.

HOW TO DRY FLOWERS

❋ Shake off any insects, but do not wash the flowers.

❋ Smaller flowers are best dried spread flat in a single layer on sheets of clean white paper, but larger flowers can be hung upside down in loose bunches tied with string.

❋ Always dry flowers in a warm, airy room away from full light.

❋ Aromatic flowers in particular need to be dried in a shady, but warm and airy place, to prevent their oils from deteriorating.

❋ When drying flowers flat, turn them frequently to make sure that they dry evenly.

❋ With plants such as LAVENDER and ROSEMARY, you can dry the flowering spikes, rather than picking off the tiny flowers separately.

HOW TO STORE DRIED FLOWERS

When the flowers are completely dry they will have lost a little of their colour and feel dry and papery. To keep them in the best possible condition follow the procedure below.

❋ Store them in glass jars with the lids well secured. Dark glass is ideal.

❋ Label jars with the content and the date.

❋ Store in a dry place, out of the light.

❋ Do not keep dried flowers for more than two years as they will gradually lose their strength.

— 3 —
Preparing Remedies

The simplest way to use flowers is to make an infusion, see opposite, with fresh or dried herbs and hot or boiling water for use as a 'tea', as a lotion, compress or eye bath, see page 33, or as an inhalation, see page 34.

Always use spotlessly clean utensils when preparing flowers. The best materials are glass for storage and enamelled pans for heating. China or pottery containers can be used for mixing and steeping preparations. Do not use plastic or aluminium.

HOW TO CONSERVE FLOWER AROMAS

When making an infusion of aromatic flowers such as LAVENDER or ROSEMARY, use hot, rather than boiling water, and be particularly careful to cover the container to keep in the volatile aromatic oils – a tea pot is ideal.

Making an Infusion

A herbal infusion for drinking and for external use is made just like tea, and is sometimes also referred to as 'tea'. Make it in a cup, or in a tea pot kept specially for the purpose.

HOW TO MAKE AN INFUSION

❋ First warm the container.

❋ Measure the required amount of the flowers into the container.

❋ Pour on a measured amount of boiling water.

❋ Cover and stand to infuse for no more than 10-15 minutes. Strain. Drink warm or cold. Many flower teas are slightly bitter – sweeten with a little honey if you wish.

❋ Unless otherwise stated, drink up to three cups daily. For quantities to use see page 32. For external application as a lotion, compress or eye bath, see page 33.

Quantities to use

Unless otherwise stated, use 1 tsp of dried flowers per cup of water.
Use two to three times the amount of fresh flowers. This is known as a
'standard infusion.' You may, however, be guided by your taste, and use
more of weak-tasting herbs and less of stronger ones.

THERAPEUTIC INFUSIONS

CHAMOMILE Use a standard infusion as a soothing eye wash or to ease
irritated skin, and as a soothing, calming drink.

ELDER FLOWER A standard infusion of Elder flowers can be drunk warm
for colds and fever, and allowed to cool for use as a complexion lotion.

EYEBRIGHT A standard infusion, strained through filter paper, makes an
excellent eye wash.

HAWTHORN (MAY) Use 2 tbsp of fresh flowers to 600ml (1 pint/2½ cups)
of water. Drink as a tonic for the circulation and for insomnia.

LAVENDER A standard infusion of flowering spikes of Lavender can be
used as a cold compress for headaches.

MARIGOLD A cold standard infusion can be used as a skin lotion.

MEADOWSWEET An infusion made with 1 tbsp of fresh flowers to a cup of
water drunk three times a day before meals is said to help cure arthritis.

YARROW The standard infusion can be used as a mouth wash for mouth
sores. An infusion made with half the standard amount can be wiped over
the skin to deter gnats and mosquitoes.

Lotions, Compresses and Eye Baths

Infusions, see pages 31-32, can be used as lotions, compresses or eye baths. They should be made in small quantities and stored in the refrigerator when not in use. Do not store for more than three days.

HOW TO PREPARE A LOTION, COMPRESS OR EYE BATH

❋ **Lotion**   Use the strained infusion when it is cool. Apply to the skin with cotton wool.

❋ **Compress**   Soak a large pad of cotton wool in the infusion and hold it to the area of the body needing treatment. Compresses may be used hot or cold. Hot compresses are reapplied as they cool and cold compresses are removed and refreshed when they have absorbed heat from the body. It helps to fold a long piece of thin (clean) cotton cloth around the pad before dipping it into a hot infusion, so that you can hold the compress by the dry ends of the cloth. Test heat before applying.

❋ **Eye bath**   To use an infusion as an eye bath, filter it through clean filter paper to ensure that no solid particles remain in the liquid and allow it to cool. Sterilize all equipment before use.

Flower Inhalations

For the treatment of head colds, sinusitis and nasal or chest
congestion the active ingredients of plants can be inhaled in steam.
This treatment is also good for the complexion.
Avoid inhalations if you suffer from asthma.

HOW TO PREPARE AN INHALATION

⁂ Pour 1 litre (2 pints/5 cups) of hot or boiling water onto about 4 tbsp of
fresh or 2 tbsp of dried flowers and leaves of flowering herbs in a bowl.
Bend over it to inhale the steam, keeping a towel over your head to
prevent it from escaping. Close your eyes and breathe in and out gently
for a minute or two at a time, over a period of about 10 minutes.

⁂ Alternatively drop up to 3 or 4 drops of the essential oil into hot water
and inhale in the same way.

INHALATIONS TO TRY

For acne BERGAMOT • CHAMOMILE • LAVENDER • ROSEMARY
For catarrh LAVENDER • ROSEMARY • VIOLET
For a cough HYSSOP • JASMINE • THYME • VIOLET
For a sore throat CLARY SAGE • HYSSOP • LAVENDER • THYME
For dull, lifeless-looking skin ANGELICA • GERANIUM • LAVENDER • ROSEMARY

Essential Oils

The essential oils are what gives a plant its scent, and they are highly valued as it takes so much plant material to yield so little oil. They are major ingredients in perfumes and are used by aromatherapists in external massage, where they are beneficial in many ways. They can make the person being massaged feel calm or revitalized, as well as helping to ease a medical complaint. Essential oils can be used at home for massage, for inhalation, see opposite, or in a bath, see page 36.

HOW TO BUY AND USE ESSENTIAL OILS

❉ Always buy from a reputable supplier.

❉ Never forget the potency of essential oils. With the exception of Lavender they are always diluted with another vegetable oil or water. Never use undiluted.

❉ Do not take essential oils internally as they can be toxic used in this way. The exception to this rule is Lavender, see pages 18-19.

❉ Unless otherwise instructed, use 5 drops of essential oil to 30ml (1fl oz/6 tsp) of vegetable carrier oil. Use 3 or 4 drops in a bowl of hot water for inhaling.

❉ Always store oils well out of the reach of children and pets.

Flower Oils in the Bath

Using flower oils in the bath is a simple and luxurious way to obtain the benefits of flowers. Add six drops of oil to the bath water after you have turned off the taps, and stir to disperse the oil.

FLOWER OILS FOR SKIN PROBLEMS

Many skin problems can be alleviated by adding essential oils of flowers to the bath water. Jasmine and Lavender are beneficial to both dry and oily skins, as they balance sebum production.

Acne BERGAMOT • CHAMOMILE • GERANIUM • LAVENDER
ROSEMARY • THYME • VIOLET • YLANG-YLANG
Dry skin CHAMOMILE • JASMINE • LAVENDER • VIOLET
Inflamed skin CHAMOMILE • CLARY SAGE • GERANIUM • HYSSOP
LAVENDER • ROSEMARY • THYME
Irritated skin ANGELICA • CHAMOMILE • CLARY SAGE • HYSSOP
JASMINE • LAVENDER • MARIGOLD • ROSE
Mature skin CLARY SAGE • GERANIUM • JASMINE • LAVENDER
MIMOSA • ROSE • YLANG-YLANG
Oily skin BERGAMOT • CLARY SAGE • GERANIUM • JASMINE
LAVENDER • MARIGOLD • ROSEMARY• YLANG-YLANG
Sensitive skin CHAMOMILE • JASMINE • LAVENDER • VIOLET

Flowers in the Home

Many flowering plants were once commonly used to keep the house clean, fragrant and pest free. Some traditional recipes are just as practical now as in the past.

TRADITIONAL POT POURRI

A pot pourri is a lovely way to enjoy the colours, textures and scents of your favourite flowers. If you make your own you can prepare a blend that gives off a completely individual fragrance.

How to make your own pot pourri

❉ Choose a selection of dried flowers for their shape, scent and colour. Pick and dry garden flowers as described on pages 28-29.
Good flowers to use: CARNATION, CHAMOMILE, CORNFLOWER, ELDER, JASMINE, LAVENDER, LILY OF THE VALLEY, MARIGOLD, MIGNONETTE, NASTURTIUM, PANSY, PEPPERMINT, PINK, ROSE

❉ Mix the petals together in a large, wide bowl. For an aromatic 'green-scented' mix, add dried herbs.
Good leaves to use: BALM, BASIL, BAY, LAVENDER, MINT, ROSE GERANIUM, ROSEMARY, SAGE

❋ To give the mixture a long life, add a fixative.
Fixatives to use: CLARY SAGE oil, powdered MYRRH, ORRIS ROOT or SANDALWOOD, bought talcum powder

❋ To round off the perfume, and give it an exotic depth, add ground spices of your choice.
Spices to use: ALLSPICE, CINNAMON, CLOVES, GINGER, MACE, NUTMEG

❋ For further scent, add a few drops of essential oil of your choice.
Do not overdo it!

❋ Store the mixture in a closed container – half-filled – for six weeks, shaking the jar frequently so that the ingredients can mix and blend.

❋ Empty into pot pourri dishes, which have lids so that the fragrance is not released too quickly, or into open bowls. Decorate the tops of open bowls with a few small Rose buds or dried Cornflowers.

Proportions to use

3 cups of dried flowers/leaves
up to 2 tbsp powdered spices
up to 6 drops of essential oil
1 tbsp fixative powder/6 drops of fixative oil

TO SCENT THE HOUSE

❋ If you grow Bay, Lavender or Rosemary, burn the cuttings from pruning in an open fire.

❋ Sprinkle a few drops of your favourite essential oil onto the fire about 15 minutes before lighting it.

TO SCENT LINEN

❋ Make muslin bags about 10cm (4in) square and fill with pot pourri mixture. Sew up the open end. Hang in the clothes cupboard or keep in linen drawers.

❋ Fill muslin bags with dried Lavender flowers and leaves and use in the same way to deter moths.

INSECT REPELLENTS

❋ Six drops of Rosemary oil mixed with 600ml (1 pint/2½ cups) of water is said to make an effective insect-repellent spray.

❋ Feverfew flowers are hated by most insects. To keep insects away, hang bunches of the flowers to dry from the ceiling.

❋ A bunch of flowering sage, hung stems upward, in a room helps to deter flies and other insects.

Bach Flower Remedies

The use of flowering plants in healing was developed in an unusual way in the twentieth century by a British doctor with a prestigious Harley Street practice in London. Doctor Edward Bach was a medical consultant, homeopath and bacteriologist, who became increasingly convinced that what lay behind the physical illness of his patients was a state of mind which drained their natural vitality and made them prey to disease.

WARNING

Although Bach flower remedies can safely be taken at the same time as conventional or alternative medicine, anyone with a serious or persistent illness is strongly advised to seek medical attention. If you are worried about any symptom, physical or mental, see your doctor.

ILLNESS AND STATE OF MIND

During his training Edward Bach observed that people who were
physically ill often seemed to be over-anxious, worrying, fearful or
impatient and he began to suspect that these emotional states were linked
to their illness. His experience as a qualified physician bore out this
suspicion, and in 1930, after over 16 years of practice, he gave up his
career in order to devote his time to studying the various harmful
emotional or mental states that encouraged bodily sickness
and to finding remedies for them.

STUDY OF WILD FLOWERS

Dr. Bach went to live and work in the beautiful English countryside on
the borders of Berkshire and Oxfordshire, seeking safe remedies in wild
flowers. His aim was to separate out the negative mental states associated
with illness and to find a single flower remedy for each. In his search, he
became attuned to a particular mental state and was then instinctively
guided to a wild plant that seemed to hold the cure to it. He then tested
out his findings by using the plant on himself, studying the effects
it had on his state of mind.

REMEDIES FOR MENTAL STATES

Dr. Bach eventually identified thirty-eight adverse mental states and a special remedy for each. The remedies are simple flower essences, and although it is possible to make them yourself, it is simpler to obtain the Bach remedies (as they are now called) ready-prepared from chemists, drug stores and health shops. This avoids the risks of causing damage to wildlife and also of using contaminated plants. As they keep indefinitely, it also means that you can have the remedies handy for use when needed.

No medical claims are made for these remedies, but there are many remarkable success stories recorded and it is said that they are effective on animals, and even plants, as well as on human beings. One thing is sure, and that is that they are harmless. You can take them while being treated by conventional or other medicine, as a further aid to recovery, or simply to remedy a particular mental state that has been troublesome in itself.

HOW THE REMEDIES ARE PREPARED

The Bach remedies use the 'essence' of the flower or plant. This can be prepared in one of two ways – the sun method or the boiling method – depending on the plant or tree material used. In each case, the flowers are picked from as many different plants of the recommended kind in the same area as possible. This ensures a variety of sources, and also that no plant is depleted of its blossoms.

SUN METHOD

Use the sun method to extract the essence of late spring and summer flowers. The flowers are picked in the morning when the sun is well up, but before mid-day, and are floated in a shallow glass bowl of spring water.

You will need

Shallow, heatproof glass bowl • Small heatproof glass or china jug
30ml (1oz) bottle and new cork • Small quantity of brandy
Bottled spring water • Label for bottle

❋ Sterilize the glass bowl, bottle and jug by placing them in a pan of cold water. Bring the water to the boil and boil gently for 20 minutes.

❋ Wrap the sterilized bowl and jug in a clean cloth.

❋ Half fill the sterilized bottle with brandy. Cork it and label it with the name of the essence to be prepared.

❋ Take the equipment to the plants you intend to use and place the bowl on level ground where it can remain in the sun for 3 hours. Fill the bowl with the spring water.

❋ Pick your flowers, holding them on a broad leaf in the palm of your hand. Place the flowers, one by one, on the surface of the water in the bowl, so that they overlap and the surface is completely covered. Make sure you do not touch the water or cast a shadow on it.

❋ After 3 hours, carefully pick off the flowers, using a stalk of a flower of the same kind, and transfer the flower water to the jug.

❋ Top up the brandy with the flower water. Cork, and store the bottle.

BOILING METHOD

The boiling method is used mostly on plant material from trees that flower in early spring. Freshly picked flowering sprays, leaves and twigs are boiled gently in spring water for half an hour and allowed to cool. The plant material is then removed, using a twig from the plant, and the liquid is allowed to stand to separate out the sediment. It is then slowly filtered into a jug through clean filter paper. Mix with brandy as for the sun method.

USING BACH REMEDIES

Study the literature published by the Bach Centre where the work of Edward Bach is still continued, before you use the remedies. Leaflets published by the Centre can be found in most parts of the world, wherever the remedies are on sale. Select the remedy for your own mental state (several can be combined) and take two drops in a cup of water as directed. Slowly sip.

The Bach Centre, Mount Vernon, Sotwell,
Wallingford, Oxfordshire OX10 0PZ, England

WARNING

Although the Bach flower remedies are safe and harmless, you must take precautions if preparing them yourself.

- Be absolutely sure that you have correctly identified the plant.
- Never use plants growing near to areas where crops are sprayed or where they could have absorbed lead from road traffic.
- Remember that many wild flowers are now protected by law so that it is a legal offence to pick them. In Britain it is against the law to uproot any wild plant.

BACH RESCUE REMEDY

As an introduction to the Remedies, try Bach's Rescue Remedy – a mixture of flower extracts for use in emergencies, after an accident, bad news, or when severely upset. Take 4 drops with 30ml (2 tbsp) of water in a glass. Many people swear by this remedy and take a bottle of the Rescue Remedy with them at all times.

— 4 —
Flower Teas

·

Flower teas are completely non habit-forming and make a pleasant change from tea and coffee. They are taken without milk and are calorie-free – unless you like to sweeten them with a little honey! However, flowers may also be mixed with Indian or China teas to give these a special lift and flavour.

Make flower teas in a tea pot as described for making an infusion, see page 31. Many individual flower teas and blends are now available in tea bags. When selecting blends, read the contents list carefully, as some contain 'nature identical' ingredients, which are not derived from flowers.

FLOWERS TO MIX WITH TEA

JASMINE FLOWERS • MARIGOLD PETALS • ROSE PETALS
VIOLET FLOWERS

SINGLE FLOWER TEAS

To clear the mind after 'the night before' and
for nervous headaches THYME FLOWER
Soothing CATMINT (CATNIP) • CHAMOMILE
LEMON BALM • LINDEN (LIME TREE)
Refreshing and invigorating BORAGE • HIBISCUS
LEMON VERBENA
Delicately flavoured CLOVER (RED) • ELDER FLOWER
ROSE GERANIUM • WOODRUFF
Tonic GROUND IVY • SPEEDWELL
Digestive SWEET CICELY and any of the soothing teas

FLOWER TEA MIXTURES

Reviving Equal parts ELDER FLOWER and PEPPERMINT
Relaxing 2 parts CHAMOMILE flowers, 2 parts ROSE petals,
1 part LEMON BALM
To lift the spirits 1 part LAVENDER FLOWERS,
2 parts LEMON VERBENA, 2 parts ORANGE BLOSSOMS

Drinks & Cordials

Flowers can be made into drinks in their own right or added to other drinks to give subtle and delicious flavours. The beneficial ingredients of the flowers are an extra bonus.

SPARKLING ELDER FLOWER DRINK

This is a lightly sparkling, refreshing drink for summer evenings

4 litres (7 pints/1 US gall) water
675g (1½ lb/3⅓ cups) sugar
8 Elder flower heads
1 orange and 1 lemon, sliced
2 tbsp white wine vinegar

Boil the water and pour over the sugar in a large, clean container.
Cover with a clean cloth. When cold add the flowers and other
ingredients. Cover again and leave for 24 hours. Strain into a
clean container, squeezing the flowers well to extract the juice.
Bottle in strong bottles. Seal well and keep for
two weeks before drinking.

Rosemary cordial wine

This is a soothing, digestive wine to drink in small glasses after a meal.
Add 4 tbsp of chopped sprigs of Rosemary to 1 bottle of white wine.
After two weeks, strain and rebottle.

Other flower-flavoured wines

Make as for Rosemary Cordial Wine, above.
For a sweet, delicate wine add Hawthorn (May) • Pinks
For a strongly flavoured wine add Hyssop • Sage

Chamomile aperitif

This is a digestive wine to sip as an aperitif.
Add 3 tbsp of Chamomile flowers and 50g (2oz/¼ cup) of sugar to a bottle
of white wine. Keep in a dark place, and gently shake each day for one
month. Strain and rebottle.

Flowers in Food

Flowers were once much more widely used in preparing food than they are now. But they can add flavour, colour and traces of extra vitamins and minerals to a range of sweet and savoury dishes.

SOME OF THE BEST FLOWERS TO USE IN FOOD

BORAGE • CHIVE FLOWERS • COURGETTE FLOWERS • ELDER FLOWERS
MARIGOLDS • NASTURTIUMS • ROSES • VIOLETS

FLOWERS FOR SALADS

DAISIES, NASTURTIUMS and BORAGE flowers are the traditional flowers to sprinkle on a mixed salad. DAISIES add a sharp, fresh, clean flavour; NASTURTIUMS give a hot, peppery taste, and BORAGE flowers add a hint of cucumber. Less well known are CLOVER flowers, which give a tangy sweetness. THYME flowers make a pretty and aromatic topping for a salad made with lightly steamed courgettes.

SAVOURY SUGGESTIONS

❊ **Chives** Flowers of chives can be folded into beaten eggs to make an unusual omelette. Serve this sprinkled with chopped chives.

❊ **Hops** The papery hop flowers can be eaten as a vegetable, gently softened in a pan of melted butter for 10 to 15 minutes. Hops are good for the digestion.

❊ **Courgette flowers** Bright orange-yellow courgette flowers may not look like food, but they are delicious dipped in a light batter and quickly deep-fried in very hot vegetable oil.

SWEET IDEAS

❊ **Rose petals** can be eaten in sandwiches made with very thinly cut bread. They also give the most delicious flavour to stewed apples.

❊ **Angelica stems** add a traditional decorative touch to cakes and custards. When bought ready prepared, they are usually coloured with green food dye. Prepared at home, the stems are pale in comparison, but naturally much better.

RECIPE FOR CANDIED ANGELICA

Cut up the stems into 5cm (2in) pieces, or less if you prefer,
and boil them gently until tender.

Drain stems and steep them overnight in a heavy syrup made by dissolving
200g (8 oz/1 cup) of sugar in 400ml (¾ pint/2 cups) of water.
Put the stems in the syrup while it is still very hot.

Dry out the stems in a very slow oven.

Skin Lotions

The skin needs regular cleansing and toning to keep it healthy. Many flowers make excellent skin-care preparations which are completely natural and easy to make. These products are best made in very small quantities and used fresh, but can be kept for a few days in the refrigerator.

FLOWER CLEANSERS

The simplest cleanser is just a strained flower infusion, see page 31, and is used warm. Experiment with the flowers listed below to find which suits you best, and try mixing two or three together. Apply the infusion or mixture to the skin with cotton wool and leave it to dry naturally. Finish by rinsing with cool water or use one of the herbal toners opposite.

BEST FLOWERS FOR CLEANSING

CHAMOMILE • LADY'S MANTLE • VIOLET • YARROW

WARNING

If your skin is sensitive avoid the use of essential oils and any but the plainest ingredients.

FLOWER TONERS

After cleansing, use a toner to remove any remaining lotion. Toners are soothing and refreshing. Use an infusion, strained, but allowed to go cold and splash it on your face to close the pores and tone the skin. Alternatively, add 1-2 drops of a floral essential oil to cold water.

BEST FLOWERS FOR TONERS

For oily skin (astringent) LADY'S MANTLE • LEMON BALM
LINDEN (LIME TREE) FLOWERS • WITCH HAZEL • YARROW
For dry skin (emollient) ELDER FLOWER • MARSH MALLOW • VIOLET
For irritated skin (healing) CHAMOMILE • LAVENDER • MARIGOLD

TONER RECIPE

For normal to dry skin 2 parts Rosewater and 1 part Witch Hazel

For oily skin equal parts Rosewater and Witch Hazel

Either splash this on the face or soak a cotton wool pad in the lotion and wipe over the face.

TONER AND CLEANSER IN ONE

An infusion of Elder flowers is both cleansing and freshening.
Use 3 tbsp of flowers to 600ml (1 pint/$2\frac{1}{2}$ cups) of boiling water, strain when cool, keep in the refrigerator and use every morning.
The mixture will last for three days kept in this way.
To keep some for later use, store it in the freezer.

—5—

A–Z for relief of common health problems

There are many tried and tested flower remedies for common health problems, and even modern 'scientific' preparations often contain ingredients derived from flowers and plants. During this century, scientists have investigated many plants to isolate their active ingredients, but medical herbalists believe that, just as it is necessary to consider the person as a whole rather than his or her isolated symptoms, it is best to use flowers and plants in their natural state as a basis for treatment.

Only the most minor problems should be treated without medical advice. Before using any of the remedies in this A-Z, turn to Using Flowers Safely on page 9. For gathering, drying and storing flowers for use, see pages 28-29 and for preparing flowers see pages 30-36.

**This A-Z should not replace visiting a doctor.
If symptoms persist seek medical advice immediately.**

BRUISES

ARNICA flowers are the standard remedy for bruises.
Use as a wash, wiped over the affected area, or a compress or in
a salve. Prepared ARNICA ointment is obtainable from
pharmacists, health and drug stores and other suppliers.
ARNICA aids rapid healing, and is equally good for sprains.

Remedy recipes

Arnica salve To make your own salve, heat 25g (1 oz) of dried
ARNICA flowers with 25g (1 oz) of lard or cocoa-butter, over
water in a double boiler, stirring from time to time.
After three hours, strain and pot in a clean glass jar.

Arnica wash or compress Use 2 tsp of dried flowers in a
cup of boiling water. Allow the infusion to cool;
strain, and use cold.

WARNING

Do not use Arnica on broken
skin. Do not take Arnica
internally except under the
supervision of a
qualified practitioner.

COUGHS

An expectorant helps to expel mucus from the lungs without the side effects of drugs. The best flower remedy for coughs is COLTSFOOT. The dried leaves are more commonly used than the flowers themselves; however, the flowers contain very similar properties to the leaves and in early spring you can pick them for immediate use.

Remedy recipe

Make an infusion of 2 tbsp of fresh COLTSFOOT flowers or 4 tsp of dried leaves to 900ml (1½ pints/4 cups) of water. Cover and steep for 30 minutes. Strain, sweeten with honey, and drink warm as required.

CYSTITIS

HEATHER stimulates the flow of urine and is a traditional French flower remedy for cystitis. Try a course of 1 litre (2 pints/5 cups) of HEATHER infusion drunk every day (by the cupful) for a month. In addition, drink plenty of water throughout the day.

Remedy recipe

Infuse 4 tsp of fresh flowering HEATHER shoots or 2 tsp of dried HEATHER in 1 cup of boiling water for 5 to 10 minutes.

DIGESTIVE DISORDERS

ROMAN CHAMOMILE has a soothing, calming, tonic effect on the whole digestive system and can safely be used for children. For diarrhoea, vomiting and colitis, try a MARIGOLD infusion. For nausea, tea made from CLOVES (the flower buds of a tropical tree), using 3 tsp to 300ml (½ pint/1¼ cups) of water, brings quick relief. A few drops of CLOVE oil can be given in water to stop vomiting.

Remedy recipes

For a Chamomile infusion use 3 tsp of fresh or 1 tsp dried flowers per cup of boiling water and steep for 10 minutes in a covered container (much of its medicinal properties are lost if the steam is allowed to escape). Drink a small cupful as required; give to children in doses of 1 tsp per half hour.

For a Marigold infusion steep 3 tsp of fresh/1 tsp dried flowers for 10 minutes in a cup of freshly boiled water.

CAUTION

For persistent digestive troubles, consult your medical practitioner.

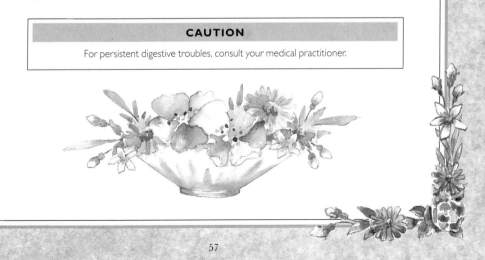

ECZEMA

Ointment made from the flower seeds of EVENING PRIMROSE is now proving to be a valuable treatment in many cases of eczema and a dietary supplement of EVENING PRIMROSE oil, which can be taken in capsule form, may also be effective. An older remedy is to apply LAVENDER oil to the skin. The freshly pressed juice of the flowering herb of CHERVIL is another traditional remedy. Salad oil in the diet can also be helpful.

Remedy recipe

Gently heat 5 tbsp of fresh LAVENDER flowers in 600ml (1 pint/$2\frac{1}{2}$ cups) of Olive oil in the top of a double boiler for two hours. Leave overnight, strain well, squeezing the oil from the flowers, and bottle. Use as required.

FEVER

A simple, but short-term, remedy for fever with a cold is to sip an infusion of BORAGE flowers. For feverishness in children, the traditional remedy is ROMAN CHAMOMILE tea, see recipe page 57. Drink plenty of cool water to replace the fluid lost in sweating.

Remedy recipe

Infuse 2 tbsp of dried BORAGE flowers in 1 litre (2 pints/5 cups) of boiling water. Cover and steep for 5 minutes. Strain and drink a cup as needed.

WARNING

FEVER IN BABIES AND YOUNG CHILDREN

If a child under the age of 6 months has a fever consult your medical practitioner AT ONCE. Also seek medical advice if fever in a child has not subsided after 24 hours.

HEADACHES

Many flowering plants can help to soothe away headaches;
CHAMOMILE, LAVENDER, PRIMROSE and ROSEMARY are some
flowers more commonly used.

Remedy recipes

Lavender oil rubbed on the temples is a remedy for migraine headaches.
For an oil rub use either 2 or 3 drops of neat LAVENDER essential oil or
LAVENDER oil, see remedy recipe opposite.

Lavender infusion can be used to treat chronic headaches.
Use 4 tsp fresh or 2 tsp dried flowers per cup of water and drink
one small cupful morning and evening.

Primrose infusion can be used to treat headaches associated with
nervous conditions or general weakness. Use 4 tsp of fresh flowers per cup
of water. Medical herbalists may prescribe an infusion of the root.

Rose petal infusion can be taken for headaches and dizziness.
Use 2 heaped tsp dried petals per cup of water.

Chamomile flower tea can soothe many types of headache.
Use 3 tsp fresh flowers or 1 tsp dried flowers per cup of water

Rosemary tea is a revivifying gypsy cure for headaches, and a pinch of
dried ROSEMARY can be added to other herbal teas. Use 4 tsp fresh
flowering tips or 2 tsp dried ROSEMARY per cup of water for ROSEMARY tea.

CAUTION

If you suffer from frequent or severe headaches, consult your medical practitioner.

INSOMNIA

Many flowers have a soothing scent which instils a feeling of relaxation and drowsiness. Try 6 drops of the essential oils of PRIMROSE, ROSE or VIOLET in a bed-time bath to induce a restful sleep. GERMAN CHAMOMILE tea, drunk in small sips before going to bed is a traditional remedy as a gentle sedative. HAWTHORN (MAY) FLOWER tea, sweetened with honey is soothing for nervous insomnia. LINDEN (LIME TREE) BLOSSOM, CATMINT (CATNIP) and HOP teas are known for their mildly sedative effect. Putting dried HOPS in your pillow-slip is another ancient remedy. Medical herbalists may also prescribe MULLEIN and ST JOHN'S WORT to aid sleep.

Remedy recipe

Make an infusion of the following flowers in the proportions given below, or vary the proportions according to your preference.
Use 25g (1oz) of dried flowers to 1 litre (2 pints/5 cups) of boiling water and steep for 10 minutes.
1 part FRAGRANT VALERIAN, 2 parts ST JOHN'S WORT, 3 parts HOPS, 5 part LAVENDER, 10 parts PRIMROSE.

Please do not pick wild Primroses, which are increasingly rare.
Primrose flowers are sometimes obtainable from specialist herbalists,
and it is easy to grow your own from seed.

CAUTION

If you suffer regularly from insomnia, consult a qualified practitioner.

NERVOUS IRRITABILITY

LINDEN (LIME TREE) FLOWER tea and GERMAN CHAMOMILE tea taken during the day and at bedtime are calming and can promote rest. (Both can safely be given to children.) A cup of ROSEMARY tea can lift the spirits and dispel depression. A few bruised CLOVES added to any herbal tea of your choice can calm irritability.

Remedy recipes
Make teas using the following quantities per cup:
Chamomile 4 tsp fresh or 2 tsp dried
Linden (Lime tree) 2 tsp fresh or 1-2 tsp dried
Rosemary 2 tsp fresh or 1 tsp dried.

CAUTION

.Rosemary is a stimulant, so do not take Rosemary tea before bed-time.

PAINFUL PERIODS

A diet containing plenty of whole foods and fresh vegetables, and plenty of exercise, especially involving gentle stretching (as in yoga) may help to prevent period pains. Drink CATMINT (CATNIP) tea as a gentle painkiller and antispasmodic if period pains occur.

Remedy recipe

Use 1 tsp of CATMINT (CATNIP) flowers and leaves to a cup of boiling water and take one cup night and morning.

SPRAINS *see* BRUISES

SWELLING AND INFLAMMATION

Swollen tissues resulting from an injury or from insect bites and stings are soon relieved by a WITCH HAZEL compress.
Distilled WITCH HAZEL is readily available from pharmacists, as a fluid extract derived from the leaves and bark of the beautifully scented winter-flowering shrub.

Remedy recipe

Dab on WITCH HAZEL lotion using cotton wool or apply as a cold compress and renew it as the heat is drawn out of the body.

INDEX

Botanical names of plants used as remedies

ARNICA *Arnica montana*
BORAGE *Borago officinalis*
CATMINT (CATNIP) *Nepeta cataria*
CHERVIL *Anthriscus cerefolium*
CLOVES *Caryophyllus aromaticus*
COLTSFOOT *Tussilago farfara*
EVENING PRIMROSE *Oenothera biennis*
HAWTHORN (MAY) *Crataegus oxyacantha, C. monogyna*
HEATHER *Calluna vulgaris*
LINDEN (LIME TREE) *Tilia europaea*
PRIMROSE *Primula officinalis*
ROSEMARY *Rosmarinus officinalis*
(Details of other flowers are given in chapter 1)